THE RUIN

MATT WILDERMUTH

RATTLING PEBBLES
NEW YORK

For
Walt and Ermengarde,
Two bright stars to herald spring.

Rattling Pebbles Press, April 2023

Many of the poems and essays within this book first appeared in the following journals and anthologies: *The Society of Classical Poets*, *Concentric Literary Magazine*, *Logos Literature*, *We've Seen the Same Horizon*, *Europa Sun*, *Terror House Magazine*, *Atop the Cliffs*, and *The Muse Commands*.

Manufactured in the United States of America
ISBN: 979-8-9881790-0-9
Library of Congress Control Number: 2023907474

CONTENTS

THE RUIN

BY MATT WILDERMUTH

THE RUIN

Keep far from us your snare,
You who lie in wait for us.
Keep far from us the time
When you will be our Coverer.
We honor you, we acknowledge your power,
But we do not desire your presence.
Take what we give you and do not return.
—Hymn to Calypso

SNOWFALL

Samite shroud
of pure white lain over the relic,
this snow the lone cover decreed
for his remains.

Restless, unwept,
his dreams move through the land;
no sickly king nor shimmering maiden
haunt but through him.

That is how things stand,
and you will soon reveal your nature,
whether you be noble or base.

Are you prepared
to join your hands with mine?
Raise with me these remains.

Winter Sketch—i

The gales of Thrace quiet no more the sea,
Nor canvas billow to drive roving souls;
Loamy earth and river's roar alike
    Sealed with the weight of winter.

Thamus ...

Wailing their idylls in the rimey grove,
The voices of decaying poets build
Their reproach, calling out to all who'll hear
    Of foul barbaric crime.

Thamus,
Are you there?

I kneel close to the fire at midnight,
A hand held to the stonework, and I listen—
Down chimney moans a lipless, tattered mouth
    In some ancient lament.

Thamus ...
When you reach Palodes ...

It is a hungry season, Ezra mine,
And I yearn to open for the shadows,
Partaking of the spirit that's released
    When a poet has died.

Take care to proclaim ...

Eastward the wind bearing a veil has come,
To enfold moonlight and lay over the earth.
Flakes dance the sky—and I must hymn once more
  An unheard truth long told.

Winter Sketch—ii

Now at the hour when gods will whisper
From their resting place within all Things
To confide with evening's softest hues,
Bathing the room in a lightness which moves
Through the most remote recesses of memory,
With a voice to uplift even the wings
Of we who yield and plummet to the earth
With a gravity of our own; at this hour, twilight,
When through eternal breath the words will throb
On unseen wires with the current of a life
Accepted at last—lived—for once truly lived,
With open eyes; yet at this awaited hour,

There is no voice, no current throbbing Things,
And no acceptance—only eyes which peer
Over the earth, over your life, and witness
The vanity—then root into the dirt.

Pale Litany

So solemn night—when a litany
Of moon inflects the snowfall with its tone;
When lowly bend attenuated branches
Enrimed, like shadowed watchmen hunching
Through the sepulcher of night; when pallid dancers
Dance to the death of the year. Have you, un-naveled
Of precedent and precept, stood with reverence
Before the chasm of the night? And there,
Seized and spanned through by such direful
Selenography—moon-struck and yielding—
Have you attended to the chorus
Of the pale light?

When first I heard its rite—
Illimitable and ancient as our blood—
It attested to my heart in such alluring
Discord. It seemed a spectral murmur
Gliding the cleft spanning between all Shapes,
Echoing of each secluded, unfamiliar
Form through the vast earth in the darkness,
Until all was anointed with this fugue
Of disharmony, unutterable
And immense. And over all the petty world
The moon intoned in somber sentence,
"Insignificant."

Snowfall

She glides forth aloft the city
On a baleful counsel of winter wind—
An ashen sea of mist flowed over the moon,
Alighting flakes which idly flit and drape
With a samite shroud our customary tableau,
Which now seem but the frailest of veilings—
Some inexpressible signifiers, dissolving.

She lies heavily like sleep over the earth—
Heaped on the church's aging steeple cross;
Hazing the iron crowns of lamppost lanterns;
Enveloping in mounds forgotten forms,
Like dolmens issuing of unnamed memory.

Such unquiet fascinations yield we here,
As, unfleshed, we're sent on ways so wide—alone.

Winter Sketch—iii

Long she wept
to the lonesome waves,
unkempt enchantress
near to the sea,

with heave and surge
of unjust spray
to douse and salt her face; and so
at last she wove a song within—

Fates conspire
as they may, never again
I'll feel this pain—but o,
lament shall he.

The Concealer

This is no dusk-lit and certain seeress
To render through your chastened eyes a glimpse—
Ungraspable and fleeting—of her secret
Grotto—that sacred place where all your
Possible selves will crest and crash like waves,
As pulsing scene gives way to pulsing scene
Until you must repent for all your debt.

Nor are her eyes the yard where as a boy
You played, and when the sun came shining down
Upon the stage of your familiarity,
Your vision throbbed and suddenly the life
Around you was disrobed and revealed—new—
And gratitude swelled to then issued forth
And suffuse the whole of creation with your love.

As her coy lips beckon you near, a whisper
From the mouth of her grotto stills your heart—
Now it is you yourself who has been disrobed—
Of you know not what—and as you look
With fascination on the crystallized
And barren relic of life, you are powerless
But to wonder—what has become of a world
Which once pulsated so with beauty,
But now seems only empty—and immense.

Leaving Ogygia i

The burdened breadth of the sea would I fathom,
Said she, before I've wrested sight of home.
Yet there—what is this mutable seaway,
These shifting waves emerging but to slip
From our aspiring eyes as yet we turn—
What's this sea before the everlasting sisters,
Whose fourteen feet glide through the night, alike
A promontory to the restless vision
Of a seafarer? Stars, luxuriant stars
Gleaming the cavern of night—and they carol
From that threshold across the aeons,
Beaming their tether of untamable song.
Like a whispering fountain of the clearest water
Is the unbowed soul as beneath their glow.
An unfathomable architecture pulses
The night, Penelope. And the one never
To dive and bathe within the uncertain sea—
The limit of the dawn and evening,
The She-Bear—port, my goddess divine.

"If in your heart you truly were to grasp
The full measure of woe it is your fate
To fulfill ere come to your native land,
You would with me abide, and keep this house,
And with me would remain immortal."

O, luxuriant the wood around
Her cave had grown—alder and aspen,
The fragrant cypress—from their eaves hymned birds

Across the spacious gardens, so tended with care.
And there from the basilica of her grotto
Stretched forth a vine, in youthful vigor blooming,
Clustered with grapes, to never wither
Or be re-born with spring. Terraced fountains
There flowed with white water, whose source defied
The grasp and reason of man—water which
Never could spill from her artificed vats
To nourish the earth. Any mortal to happen
There would gaze ever-more in admiration,
And in his mind stay wrapped with wonder—

Never to witness wither and then shed
This ephemeral and wavering vessel;
Never to hear murmur the water
Of my unaided days from this amphora,
Pouring to harmonize with the countless remnants
Of all who have returned to the vast sea;
A changeless effigy of he who was.

Seventeen days on the sea sailed he ere
The shadowed mountains of the Phaeacians
Emerged, resembling—where nearest—a shield
From the mist which churned upon the waters.

Winter Sketch—iv

Within the vastness of the brumal prairie—
A place of brittle grasses and bald shrubs,
Where the low wood makes moan and rivers still—
A cragged visage, recumbent, has emerged
From the earth to glare into the heavens.
Summiting his knit brow, one can't help
But look upon this once-familiar tract
As stripped of some context—irreparably—
And stare in disbelief.

Winter Sketch—v

Now angelic choirs no more to man resound,
  Wraiths moan the earth to which he's bound,
To sing of wounds with vengeance that would bring
  Actaeon to Diana by the spring.

Winter Sketch—vi

Bitter berries,
lip-red in a quilt of snow,
your holly leaves have fallen
long ago.

Shying your welcome
from briar thorn and sullen field,
too few the lips to look on you
and yield.

Yet when in driving wind
and drifted snow his path is lost,
Only a fool would pass you by,
anxious of the cost.

The Blind Poet

I

It was my twenty-fourth year when I first lost the ability to see—to truly see. I had already written a great many poems, but each impression, each depth of feeling which welled forth in the urge to compose lines of verse, found itself swallowed by something I did not yet understand; something which, while engulfing my work, drew me, myself nearer and nearer its eager mouth. Approaching this void—what apter epithet may we offer that devouring fiend within, nihilism—chaos and uncertainty rendered me useless to understand why my poetry had failed.

By the next year, my twenty-fifth, I knew something wicked had me in its grasp.

II

That so few of our nation's poets emerge from Ohio should astound—so arresting are its forests and streams for the sensitive youth. Yearning for adventure, I would wander my state's nature preserves and countryside, washed over by a kaleidoscope of impressions. The secret meadows, the springs and streams, the forsaken campgrounds, and the lonely coppices all seemed to possess something beyond mere beauty: something more essential, holy, and unique to each form—and I was a joyful child, turning the cylinder to witness it all. Gradually, however, this animistic magic ceased to pour into my vision and soon my life-long yearning for the woods resolved.

As my fascination with life continued to wane, unfamiliar thoughts rushed over the horizon of my consciousness. I had hoped to revive an art form suffering a century of failure and, by doing so, aid a broader movement to recover a culture in dire decline. Yet I wondered why a people, an art, or even myself mattered before the vastness of not only our own world but the infinitely vast, teeming universe. A universe, furthermore, within some even broader context of unimaginable time. And this vastness, it seemed to me, lacked any intrinsic value or transcendent quality. Men of the past centuries needed but to turn to the Church and thus dissolve the dark spell of existential despair—if such magic were encountered at all. For modern man? The procession of Columbus and Copernicus, Galileo and Kepler, Bacon and Descartes, Hutton, and Darwin, and finally Planck, Rutherford, and Bohr had deprived us long before of these guiding lampposts of the past. In the age of reason, could one believe—truly believe—in the literal truth of the Bible, as Christians insist one must? Contemplating the Church, I found myself eager to accept a holy Father and even a savior who had appeared to us to share his profound spiritual truths. But that Jesus had truly, in reality, walked on water? That God had truly, in reality, parted the Red Sea?

Must it not be that we had misread these spiritual truths into mere dogmatism—and thus sapped them of their revelatory essence? Yet where else to turn for guidance?

III

During this period of aesthetic collapse, I shared a townhouse with a singer and budding socialite. On many weekend nights, my friend would hold parties in our parlor for local musicians, writers, artists, and intellectuals. Compelled out of friendship to attend, I would converse with this would-be local elite and encounter many ideas against which I hoped to later wage war. One such night I sat in my chair, rather apart from the crowd and disinterested in conversation. I instead watched and listened, attempting to engage the poetic vision that had fled me. We may savor any mundane moment at all, I once knew, in the same manner in which we enjoy a work of art: as captivated, detached observers, disinterested in any outcomes and thrilled merely to sense. And at that moment, I found again the same nothing which had robbed me of my thrill in the countryside. The faces of party-goers, the lighting and shadows of our home left no lasting impression. The roll of conversation and the sweep and thud of shoes on hardwood all came to my ears absent of their former music. I could sense nothing.

Seized by desperation, I abandoned the party and fled upstairs to the privacy of my room. After throwing the books from my bed, I found a recording of Wagner's *Tristan und Isolde*. I then shut off the light and drew the bedding over my eyes so that I might more easily enter one of my most beloved regions—the realm of music.

As Wagner's triumph of passion swelled in "inexhaustible repetitions" arranged so masterfully to incite within the listener that same insatiable fervor of Tristan for Isolde, I recalled my own experience of love and its tragic end; I recalled the loss of my childhood home; I recalled the thrill which had seemed to pulsate the world before that time—and I *pushed* some inner power, willing myself to feel—to feel anything, anything at all, even loss, even pain—and I, the poet, could sense nothing at all but quiet disinterest in that same music before which Giuseppe Verdi "stood in wonder and terror," and knew that I was lost. Seven years would pass before I composed another poem.

Prospero

His tome cast to plunge and fade to subtle worth
In precious fragments faint, he paused to glean,
Then clear, what lucid phantom rendered forth
Of the deep blue imager's stilling sheen.

The Ruin

Those days have departed, and the world is not
As once it was. Dormant the vines now lie,
And frost is on what barren stalks yet show;
An immense silence besets the heart with cold,
And the dim sun, so like a songless moon,
Wanly its gleam bestows.

O Radegund,
Fallen, fallen our temples lie. Though columns
Yet aspire to mantle dawn, their archways
Sprawl the dirt. Charted aisles compel,
Only to terminate in rubble—while
Path-maker chance his unknown marvels will heave
Out of the hidden land. The roofs have fallen,
And when into the bared luster of dusk
The sun has plunged, and night has arched her back
To caress the earth with her secret gleam, then
All mankind must plunge itself through mist
Of an unknown twilight dimness. Hardly may one
But cast a backward glance to look but once
Upon all we have lost. Not Troy alone
Must her ruins mourn, indeed.

Yet was the sainted
Princess compelled in all her loss, as we,
Like some lost Hecubas, to look in wonder
On the fractured tablet of what was the sun?
And not a thousand prayers, nor even rounds
Of Patroclus' tomb will raise again

The eternal gardens past, lapsed from the soul
In the winter.

Though in our secret hearts
An unknown voice through the snowfall may cry,
'All is naught; all is lost,' there is a beauty
In the soft glow of the wan sun when on
The reaped and wintered fields it shines, if one
Still has the heart to dream.

Saint Radegund, princess of Thuringia, c. 520-587 AD. In 531, Chlothar I of the Franks invaded her pagan kingdom in a war of conversion. Chlothar made the captured princess one of his six concubines. Radegund detailed this invasion in a piece we have come to know as *The Fall of Thuringia*, from which the following is selected:

Oh, sad state of war, malevolent destiny
That fells proud kingdoms in a sudden slide!
Rooves that stood so long in happiness are broken
To lie fallen beneath the vast charred ruin.
The palace courts, where art once flouished
Are vaulted now with sad, glowing ashes.
Towers artfully gilded, then shone golden-red,
Now drifting ashes blur the glitter to pallor.
The captive maid given to a hostile lord, her power fell
From the heights of glory to the lowest depths.
The conquering flame belching, reddens the gold hair
of her beloved
While the milk-white woman lies on the ground.
Alas, the corpses lie shamefully unburied on the field,
An entire people, strewn in a common grave.
Not Troy alone must mourn her ruins:
The Thuringian land suffered equal slaughter.
The matron was rapt away, with streaming hair, bound fast
Without even a sad farewell to the household gods.
Nor could the captive press a kiss on the threshhold
Nor cast one backward glance toward what was lost.
A wife's naked feet trod in her husband's blood
And the tender sister stepped over the fallen brother.
I, the barbarian woman, seek not to count these tears,
Nor to keep afloat in the melancholy lake of all those drops.

Interlude on the Art of Poetry i

For Dr. Williams, regarding his unfortunate misdiagnosis.

There are those rare voices among us making moan—not with the freshness of a spring breeze, but rather with the sterility of a winter wind—of the need for a great return to a Golden Age passed; "we must go back" is their rallying cry—who would have us crawling through barrows only to return with the brittle bounty of *Lyrical Ballads*—the bones of one long-dead. Such poets may think themselves akin to Strabo's "diviners by the dead" who, through discourse with ancestral spirits, were said to attain guidance and wisdom, but to my mind, their work seems to speak more of hooded figures around a fire-pit at the witching hour, raising corpses to write "parchèd" rather than "parched."

The spirit of a time, the vitality with which our great masters lived, the multifarious zeitgeists of ages lapsed—these are as much our ancestors as the words upon a page, read without precedent. Who today can truly "sing of the progresse of a deathlesse soule" in the voice of Donne without—for shame—seeming inauthentic, however heartily he may try? Great achievements are birthed of the vitality of the individual—are, in fact, the individual. Our art consists of much more than the clever arrangement of words according to tested standards and ye olde time voice and rhyme.

And yet—rise, Nietzsche!—oh, my foes and ah, my friends, "I will not be mixed up and confounded with others." Think me not one of the tarantulas of poetry—those acolytes of our cultural winter, the postmodernists. They live yet, and no denials nor misdirections will serve to hide that fact, Mr. Foucault.[1]

Still, the voice of spring within our ancestral spirit returns today through that self-same "met-him-pike-hoses" of all ages—and winter does have its say, does it not? The meter creeks when we stand. The low mimetic mode is tighter than one may wish at this age.[2] Our spirit, our voice, has suffered a hardship rarely reckoned in the annals of history—and, anyway, spring is not the exact return of conditions lapsed. Spring blossoms forth anew, reconciling and redeeming the hardships of winter. Regin reforged Gram, the sword of Sigurd's father, not by stepping through a rift in time discovered at the rear of a diner's storage closet, to then revisit the days of yore, but rather, Regin forged—in present time, with present materials—a blade with the sharpness to, as floating upon the Rhine, slice in twain a drifting hank of wool.

Spring approaches, rearing change. The postmodernists are not of spring. What Wife-of-Bath-energy to engender the gain of crisp buds may we read in such meek lines as offered by Emily Wilson in her celebrated translation of Homer's rhapsody—

> Tell me about a complicated man.
> Muse, tell me how he wandered and was lost
> when he wrecked the holy town of Troy.
> And where he went, and who he met.

1 **Foucault**. Oh, we're equal, Georgie. We're all equal down here.
2 **low mimetic mode**. From *Poem Shape*, occasionally an insightful blog: "Low mimetic writing deals with the life of ordinary people, with the everyday life we live, seen from the inside, where the mythic and high mimetic modes treat the life of heroes and kings, seen from the outside."
In poetry this generally translates to writing in the voice which one uses during a casual conversation over mimosas at brunch.

Why precisely is this work celebrated? Because it lowers. These poets, critics, and philosophers ask us to not till nor sow again the bounty of the earth; they, seedless, ask us rather to defile. We must discard the fervor of our lapsed arts and philosophy, we are told, for they do not speak with the new voice of a new people emerging from dens of fantisful sleep in ignorance—from the fantasies of aesthetic standards, of the striving for truth, of such antiquated ideas as beauty and divinity. "The fight is on," William Carlos Williams wrote. "These men who have had the governing of the mob through all the repetitious years resent the new order."

Winter's sun so chills the heart that we adapt to regard summer itself oppressive, do we not?

Dr. Williams is correct, of course, but misdiagnoses the malady: if that writing heralded today as the only possible achievement were presented with the brilliance of the sun's rise upon early spring . . . but what did Williams offer us?

> What about all this writing?
>
> O "Kiki"
> O Miss Margaret Jarvis
> The backhandspring
>
> I: clean
> clean
> clean: yes . . . New-York
>
> Wrigley's, appendicitis, John Marin:
> skyscraper soup—

This? This is the poetry of life? Of *spring itself*?[3] Yet if there is something the bunglers of the last century have yielded us, it is the fulfillment of ancient prophecy:

> Hard is it on earth, | with mighty whoredom;
> Axe-time, sword-time, | shields are sundered,
> Wind-time, wolf-time, | ere the world falls;
> Fast move the sons | of Mim, and fate
> Loud blows Heimdall, | the horn is aloft,
> In fear quake all | who on Hel-roads are.
> Yggdrasil shakes, | and shiver on high
> The ancient limbs, | and the giant is loose . . .

The emptying of the poetic line, the lowering of the voice, the butchering of the poetic image: we may read all this as a calamity—and it is so—but what is the spirit-message of the black sun when into the sea the land sinks at last?

> She sees, coming up a second time,
> earth from ocean, eternally green;
> the waterfalls plunge, an eagle soars above them,
> over the mountain hunting fish.

Yet spring first renders forth not in the fullness of magnolia blossoms to freshen the lane with a sweet scent and a shower of pink petals, rather with slender shoots, unadorned, green with the juice of life. Shakespeare is of summer—

> Good Hamlet, cast thy nighted color off,
> And let thine eye look like a friend on Denmark.
> Do not for ever with thy vailed lids
> Seek for thy noble father in the dust:

3 And this from *Spring and All*, the book in which Williams proclaimed the dawn of a cultural spring—in the year of our Lord 1923. The good doctor went so far as to offer his own work—this poem included—as example of this new age of artistic bounty. Have ye no shame, ye base defilers?

Thou know'st tis common; all that lives must die,
Passing through nature to eternity.

These words issue not of such chaotic seas as drift we. Yet might we do better than Ashberry? According to the professor and critic Langdon Hammer, "no figure looms so large in American poetry over the last 50 years as John Ashberry." Yet one cannot read Ashberry's verse without wondering from whence this esteem has risen.

Let's try the ingenuous mode, if for no better
Reason than its staying power: locked into a continuum
That rises and falls with the countours of this earth,
Inhabiting Tom Tiddler's ground of special pleading
and cash-and-carry. Long lines at the checkout counter
Are a reason to behave.

In reading Ashberry's first collection, Auden famously confessed that he "hadn't understood a word" of the manuscript. In fact, Ashberry's work seems little more than a stream of non sequiturs which, individually, provide slight hints at an inclination and, when forced together into his irregular lines, communicate nothing in particular. In even the most fundamental analysis, the above excerpt fails: it is, first and foremost, nonsensical; it consists of no regular meter; the lengths of its lines are not predetermined by any discernible structure; and the personal implications of his ramblings amount to the blandest mundanity. It is wholly a poem without sense, and this must be said of nearly all our postmodern poetry.

But, they say, —why do you not write in the common language of women and men? And why make use of such outdated concepts? I couldn't read your poems with my morning coffee. Meter? What are you, some kind of racist? Your footnotes fail to follow official MLA guidelines. What the hell are you even saying? You have set poetry back centuries.

I take all of this to mean—yes, hello again, Dr. Williams— —you have not comforted me for my lack, nor for my sin. You have asked me to read carefully and to consider. I have a Facebook notification and you are in the way. I like Rupi Kaur. She is as digestible and warm and disposable as a pumpkin spice latte.[4]

The wind began to howl horribly the other day. I dared not approach the window for fear of looking into the eyes of that blood-stained guardian at Hel's gate. Oh, was it fierce. But I recall last winter. Not long before our Herewearagain Gaities lead us a ricorso round to the Cross and then people forgot it. There was a fierce wind, just like the one I'm telling you about now. It howled so badly it woke the children and they cried. It was the worst storm of the winter, but the last before spring. The last. Could it be otherwise? ... As Housman's "weeping Pleiads" wester, the sun draws near the horizon. We hardly hear Yeats' rattle of pebbles at this point. Winter's worst throes soon will pass and we, or our grandson's grandsons, will drink of life again. For now, what may we, the Created Uncreating (if we are indeed an aspect of Nature), desire to fashion? Ultimately? The Uncreated Creating's great gift: the Created Creating. And if this seems like a paradox, you're well on your way.

4 One of Rupi's best poems from *Milk and Honey* according to *The Atlantic*:
"i thank the universe
for taking
everything it has taken
and giving to me
everything it is giving"
That's it. That's the poem. Were I a money-making sort of man, I would write such a collection over a few relaxed weeks and call it *ur enough*, by Leticia Jackson.

Winter Sketch—vii

A song prevails in spring not present
This lingering term; it blows along magnolias
To toss their hanging bloom; it births in time
The hatchling and rears the fresh-grown shoot;
It appeals to the winter-worn and aged,
To lighten their hearts anew, with not the hymn
Of indifferent allure, but the timeless strain
Of awe, which abides in youth.

This reverent tone,
Inspiriting all, lays the themes of the bloom's
Bold seize of engendering plots, to develop
In summer, then counter in fall. May it not
Restate in what bars the winter wind allots?

Winter Sketch—viii

What music here softens no more the austere
And pitiless span of the prairie,
Yet music there is. Casting forth of itself,
The winter too finds voice—in the sealed creek
And budless shoots.

As murmurs this bleak air
Through the hills, also it pleas through the heart—
Could not the spring, and hope, and even love,
Within such seasons as these, seem no more
Than a refuge of our tenuous fantasy?

THE GARMENTS OF CALYPSO

I

Thus the book of the madness of an age—
And I think of the trembling voice,
The bewilderment, the dread of Kafka,
He who perhaps surpassed us all in pure
Embodiment of the time—and he a ...
But that should be of no surprise now.
I think of Eliot and the fire and rose
Which are one. He who was content to wait,
By all accounts fastidious, for what else
May he have done? And how could he have known
What the fools would do with him? And I think too
Of Pound, whose reply, if made at all, was lost
Within the the fathomless portent of braying waves,
Which, lash upon lash, blasted remnant spires—
His crumbling sentinel 'liths yet unbowed—
The great chronicler, legislator,
And prophet lost to ugly madness.

II

Soon pale day-break, and then the brittle herbage
Beneath our walnut bough, a filthy crust
Of snow along the drive, and an ice shelf
Too cold to melt with salt; the unsettling hurry;
The plowed walkway; din of truck and car and bus;

Smog and, perhaps, the hoarfrost, and somewhere,
Distant, forgotten—the prairie. But now the peace
Of night, the ascent of my smoke through the chimney,
And disquiet thoughts I welcome only now.

III

I would not laugh and offer comfort
With labyrinthine promises as Joyce,
For all is not so sure as once it seemed.
And Spengler, to whom all present and active
Was once clear and yet to whom the future was
As veiled as all must seem to we persisting,
Is neither my true purview nor my cause;
Nor may I slip my vision into the night
To glide through the rooms and the spirits
Of a people to catalog with loving eyes,
As the American bard wandered long.

O yet—be with Tiresias and Cassandra
And what powers within may still persist—
To guide my vision and release my voice
To speak with truth of the garments of Calypso
And the fraught voyage from Ogygia ...

Faust's Bedchamber

Faust stokes a dying fire while Gretchen removes her jewelry and prepares for bed.

Faust [Aside.]
There was a time, feeble flame, when to pour forth
Your spirit into all Things and so gleam
Even this meager chamber with a light,
Not merely by which one may clearly see,
Nor warm himself by the flames thereof,
But, God, to glow to life the very room
As though with the sacred spirit of all fire
You'd set to flame each form with endless
Mystery and unending beauty,
And no curtain nor armchair idly sat,
But burned within the soul—and now no more.
And so I, failing flame, yes, and so I.

Gretchen [Aside.]
And where, my love,
Do you depart?
Where are the eyes
That sought my art?

How far they roam
From their true home
Within the warmth
Of my heart.

No more his eyes
When they depart

Will seek their end
Within my heart.

How far they roam
From their true home
Within the chambers
Of my heart.

O, Faust, my Faust,
To where do you depart?

FAUST [ASIDE.]
O that you would return once more, my flame

GRETCHEN [ASIDE.]
No more will you
Return to me

FAUST [ASIDE.]
Banish this shadow from over my eyes.

GRETCHEN [ASIDE.]
To take your warmth
With only me.

FAUST [ASIDE.]
And let me look upon the truth once more.

GRETCHEN [ASIDE.]
O look on me
With need once more.

A rapping at the door disturbs their silence.

GRETCHEN
He's come again!

Faust

Who? Someone is knocking,
So let them in.

Gretchen

Oh, I would not, my love.
I do not trust the man. No, it is he,
Who else would call at this late hour? He's come to ...

Faust

Don't be hysterical. We have a guest.

Knocking from the hall continues as
Faust takes a candelabra and moves to open
The door, which unbolts as though on its own.
Mephistopheles enters the room.

Ah, yes, it is you after all, old friend.
But what at this hour brings you to my door?
You see, the fire dies and we ready for bed.

Mephistopheles

Faust! By thee invited! Surely
You would not believe your plea unheard
By such as me. And, behold, I have come.
Would you receive your answer? Ask me,
And I shall reveal to you the truth.

Gretchen

Turn him out! Close your ears to his deception
And look to me, dearest. I've seen a distance
Wash over your eyes like you look on some
Remote horizon known only to you.
Look on me, love—is it not love, you've said
That is the tinder of philosophy,
That if one only looks to his beloved

The flame that there ignites can't help but spread
Forth into all things and to all of life,
Until creation's whole emblazens with
The Truth of the Lord? Look on me, my Heinrich.

MEPHISTOPHELES
She speaks the truth, but you know well a sober
Real, a dictate as of His own will—
We may not see things as they are, but merely
As we are. Would you know the truth, my friend, and see
With shining eyes once more?

FAUST
Yes, I would know.

Thus MEPHISTOPHELES raises his hands
To FAUST's chest and with waving fingers
Draws forth an orb. Clouds churn its surface
And roll over his fingers. From its depths
An intimate light glows and pulses.

CHORUS OF ANGELS AND EARTHLY SPIRITS
O, man, your Christ waits not,
For he has never left!
His Joy persists in all,
And His blood throbs the earth!
So blaspheme not against
The Holy Ghost, O Man!
For sacred is this life.

MEPHISTOPHELES
Name for us all you see, as best you may.

FAUST
It is self-luminous and fixed, yet moving
And pulsing with the motions of the heart.

The heavens and earth, the sun and moon,
And all the stars seem to stir within
This one sphere. Never have I seen a rival
In beauty to this one gem in your hands...

MEPHISTOPHELES
You speak well, yet there is more you must see.

Then looking as one whose reluctant duty
It is to bestow burdened knowledge
Upon a soul heedless of trials to come,
With riving fingers he pulls the sphere in twain.
GRETCHEN makes the sign of the cross as
MEPHISTOPHELES bestows the orbs
Upon FAUST, whose hands tremble as they reach.

MEPHISTOPHELES
And now?

FAUST
My eyes are drawn to one whose light
Shines as only heaven's light may shine.

CHORUS OF ANGELS
Kneel ye before the Lord of Heaven,
Tis He who stands beyond the earth!
Tis He whose works surpass the known,
And move beyond the unknown!

Build ye your towers, man, and see
How swift they fall before His will!
You build your towers, man, to see
A form beyond the scope of thee.

So as the faultless sun may shine
A faultless light which never dies,

O man you are His moon to mirror
A borrowed light which once was clear.

FAUST

Dawn mantles the sky and yet the earth remains
Within a slumber as of night. And now—
I behold in the sky a cleft which spreads.
Crossed bars of light alike a grievous passage
To His eternity! O Lord, forgive
My eyes.

MEPHISTOPHELES

You sound unlike yourself, dear Heinrich.

FAUST

This light is unobtainable. I can
But yield and kneel before its glory!

As the light of this sphere burns ever brighter,
The forgotten second sphere begins to dim.

This other sphere which, when the two were one,
Had glown with the most holy of all light
Has softened near extinction. Now as I
Look once again, it is as though my vision
And the orb are united in some mystic
Harmony, for its light advances fast.

CHORUS OF EARTHLY SPIRITS

Sweet are the songs of children,
Dear lambs whose hopes and fears
Like gentle rainfall shower
To nourish with their power;

And not the stalking fox nor rising fern
Flourish but run like dreams from their own urn.

And when youth's storms have passed
We see at last the truth—
All we've hoped, all we've feared
Have only in our minds appeared.

From dust to dust, from nought to prime,
Our life a moment brief—forgot in time.

So rainfall shower
Unto the bower;
Our truths are ripples to soon recede,
And heaven and hell are but a creed.

O man is droll,
His bell will toll
And on his grave will sop the rain,
Yet never will he think that he is vain.

Faust

I see a fog over the world, quickly dispelled;
A searing light: a god—no, but a star;
And wills at war, taking their mates by the sea;
Now a realm hidden within all the world,
Of endless mystery, shunning measurement!
Yet all the images have altered—
I see suspended in darkness the forms
Of man's desire and reason! The soothing mask;
A child, secretive and hiding at play;
The stern father; the welcoming arms of the mother—
And all revolving around men and women
So laughably heedless of the influence
Of these rotating imagers of psyche!
So pitiful and helpless seem these men.
To think they traverse with firm steps about
The globe, directing with clear eyes its turning,
All the while inattentive to the truth

Of their impotence before such powers.
Dismal and sad is the state of these men!
If not for disgust I would mourn their fate.
Yet now, O God, dear God, standing among
The helpless masses—with fearful, unknowing
Eyes reeling—my own self! No, all is nought,
All is lost. What have you done to me?

At this the vision and light of this orb vanish.
Unbeknownst to Faust in his narration,
The light of his room has dispersed as well
To leave a lone beam cast on he alone,
While both GRETCHEN and MEPHISTOPHELES
Have disappeared. And so in darkness,
His frantic and despairing eyes begin
To turn from one orb to the other,
Yet neither will enflame nor share their visions.
Thus FAUST determines to rid himself of
The orbs but cannot shake them from his hands.
At last he falls onto the floor and weeps.
The bedroom light returns as Faust's light fades
And GRETCHEN finds herself alone in the chamber.

GRETCHEN
O Faust, my Faust, to where do you depart?

The Theologian's Dream

I

I stand on a cragged shelf
which juts from mountainside
over the valley.

And devise once more my descent
to that place of cloaked herbage
and virile darkness.

For in that valley rests
a lake I've looked upon
these many nights.

The cool, mysterious
waves of water call
to me again.

And yet despite my want
to plunge both hands and drink
of those depths,

I have not pardoned
my feet to seek the shore.
I know not why.

So many nights distracted
and hindered by my fear—
but no more.

II

Beyond such meager glow
as moonlight streams my path—
murky night.

Desperate faces seek
through that gloom, wandering
without design.

Their lamentations thrum
and trouble through the air
with bewildered woe.

Then at my back, heavy feet
drag at the dirt as though
burdened by hardship.

I turn—into the moonlit path
there limps a hunchbacked creature,
shuffling toward me.

A fissure mars his face
from crown to chin between
afflicted eyes.

Mortal terror wells
as his arm rises slow,
then points to me.

But I refuse to falter
in my pursuit—and so run
for the dark lake.

As distance spreads between
the creature and myself,
I hear him yawp

and mumble in a voice
both incomprehensible
and desperate.

III

At last my path through clearing
from those black woods has lead
to the lake's repose.

Crests lave the pebbled strand
at my approach; the air
is crisp and rank.

Firm shingles receive
my knees with flagellation;
pain sweet as wine.

I lower my hands to lade
a drink as the swell rushes
upon my thighs.

Then far off over the span
an unseen breath exhales
on the dark water.

The lake shudders and heaves
under the moan of wind—
o terrible moan!

Whose voice would sound with force
to heave the world? Who to shock
and shake the deep?

What spirit had awoken
in this dark place of wonders?
And who may tell me?

And what courage courses man
to sustain through such hell
of desperate fear?

I scrambled from the water
yet knew flight could achieve
no escape.

The water, the dark water,
rushed over the revolting
flesh of my hands.

And as a final shudder
raced up my back, I screamed—
and at last awoke.

Minos

I

For we, the wealth and glory of lapsed kings—
Eager women, well-bred through untold
Centuries of a noble lineage—
Unending knowledge and its dissemination—
And the white bull to secure our reign.
In our hands lies all to which man may aspire.

II

I wake from fearful dreams and know not why.
Horror echoes down the halls of night—
A bellow, thundering hooves, and a cruel pant
Exhaled over my soul. Rolling eyes
Searching without rest, searching for—for me.

Helgi Hjörvarðsson

Alone he sat, the one called the Silent Man,
Upon a barrow forgot to all but he.
Here, where the endless words at last began
To quiet in his heart—here, where he could see
The restrained barrier between known and unknown
Broaden to plunge itself into all things,
Spreading a great sigh of wordless peace—a stone
Upon which he may rest, and where there sings
Nothing but the speechless birds and stream,
Where his mind is free at last to merely dream.

As he sat so at rest, nine Valkyries
Flew over the lea near to his mound;
Of these there was one who seemed sent to seize
His heart, so noble and fair he at once found
The maiden's visage and form. His searching eyes
Locked upon hers. At once she flew to him
And spake: "Late will thee, Helgi, king, arise
To seize rings and shining fields—the eagle screams the rim
Of sky soon—yet long, my idle king, must you seek
If you've not the will to give thought form—and speak."

Ysätters-Kajsa

I

Where sags the sun in its refrain
To pour its gleam on glassy sea;
Where lacteal pink in sky and deep
Will merge upon the doubling main;
Where plaited at the circlet fringe,
Twin orbs will sear where one had sank,
A storm released one day in fury,
Diffusing in its neutral hue
Across the orbs and dappled gloss,
Advancing from the horizon.

Barrows upon the ocean swelled,
Cresting to spill sea back to sea,
Which, heaving, mounted higher,
Each wave then birthed of wave before.
A breath over the brine exhaled,
As spread the brume from sea to shore,
Dispensing of itself the while,
Drawing adown in languid threads
To dissolve to the seaway gray.

And at a promontory
Where wave upon wave lashes rock,
The wind began to moan and rush,
Disturbing trees to shudder,
Then swept from headland down to plain.

II

Observing the vale in winter luster,
As eddied wind through grasses sighed,
There sat young Himinglæva
Within her home upon the hillside,
Lonely above the lowland vale.
And ever lonely dwelled the girl,
Idly awaiting a reprieve
From her exacting mother,
Impoverished and husbandless,
And from the ceaseless burdens
An elder sister always bears.
But few idle and lonely pleasures
Did she take, walking where a stream
Through the forest coursed in summer
Toward the solitary marsh,
Alighting in winter
What places apart she may find
Within the home her mother made.
And neither would a husband take she,
Though all attractive men of youth
Would offer her their eager hand,
And each careful entreaty
By such men all girls have desired,
And each appeal her mother offered
To return her to the travails
Daily compelled by home and hearth,
Each of her sisters' needful pleas,
All only served to agitate
The thunderous pounding within,
Where longed her vestal heart for flight.

So sat she near to the window,
Housework undone and spindle shunned,
When the wind came to murmur.
A gray lament suppressed the twilight

As the vast storm outstretched its hand
From the sea through the frigid plains,
And what birds, wintering, remained,
Dusted the snow in their retreat
To refuge in the storm-braced firs.
All of the vale at once was livid
With an anticipation.

And the wind glided to the girl,
Approaching her home on the hillside,
Longing with soft words to be near,
To toss amongst her flying hair,
And caress down her pearly skin.
Though her coy fingers to the pane
Approached to graze a biting frost,
A flame had lit within her heart
When the voice of her mother called,
"Himinglæva, come from there;
The house must now be readied.
A storm is blowing from the sea.
The shudders must be latched and braced,
The chickens gathered to their coup!"

These words upon her fell like stone,
As from her life's horizon
Advanced the days ahead her,
When never again would the woman,
When woman at last she would be,
Never would she elated dance
Amongst the springtide blossoms,
Artless and free as when a girl;
When never song would sing of spring,
To draw her to the florets near
As the clean breeze blew through her hair;
When no more would life as a song be;
When she would clean, and cook, and care,

And at days end at last would breathe,
Only to sleep a dreamless sleep.
Fury within her chest came swelling,
And a truth exhaled over her heart.
Then away from the window
She turned to face her mother,
And looked upon her sisters,
As pity then at last released
In tears for those she'd ceased to love.
With one last look did she flee.

III

The shutters of her home slammed shut
In the wind's frenzied buffeting.
The sky was now beyond a glimpse,
Obscured within the quickened snow.
Not a voice could she distinguish
As she scrambled down from the hillside
Within the storm's subduing clamor,
Shaken and lost so near to home.

Yet as she ran into the field
A calm awakened in her heart,
When waves of wind around her teased,
Ascending in a hurried joy
To billow and to pull her dress;
To caress and lash at her face;
To rebound and tug her flowing hair.
Her pallid arms began to hover,
Gliding to dance like rushing water,
As she began to turn in fearful
Rapture, releasing with the wind
Over the prairie to the sky,
Like water from an amphora pouring;
And gossamer became her skin,
As the tossed snow upon the plain;

And light as air became she then,
Diluting in the rushing gale,
Until at last her spirit thinned,
And vanished was her body;
Vanished in wind to flow at last,
As the release of rising smoke
An offering will issue
Through the sun-door of a longhouse,
Himinglæva was no more.

Epigrams on Nøkken

With virtuous eyes and with flowing hair,
She draws men near to watch them gasp for air.

Supple and fond within the river's flow,
The touch desired so, so drags men to woe.

Hushed are her eyes and fond; so welcoming her arms;
All death and all delight are the promise of her charms.

Lithe in the water, nøkken with lovers unite.
And the men as they drown call out, "delight, delight!"

Pale as the moon upon the river's shrift,
Swimming nøkken play—where their lovers drift.

Interlude on the Art of Poetry ii

Welcome to the annual Poetic Universality-Sculpting Symposium yield, in which we aim to disseminate with the subversive power of the pantoum and the wingspan of the sonnet a discussion of this year's compendium of observations on poetry in the year 2022. We begin with the poignancy of Mxr. Raheem Nair on the science of perception.

Distinguished in its sincere and unbroken
attention toward the logistics of experience,
the opening statement provided
by Mxr. Nair makes the bold claim that
it is essential in the postcolonial market
to address hwhite plagiaristic dissemination
of minority voices.
Through the analytics of historical retrospectivism,
Nair claims,
We see in the works of R. Rosenbaum, Evelyn Greene,
And Taika Waititi
That just because
something
is bad doesn't
mean that
it is bad.
Which is, of course, the heteronormative zeitgeist.
So. What does that mean
if this is, in truth,
factually relevant?
The science isn't finished.

I

As Mx. Rosenbloom states
as a preclause
to their thesis
on Othello,
The dualism of the poetic line
is clearly, if one follows the reasoning of Georg Wilhelm Friedrich Hegel,
a restraint upon
non-privileged
voices.
                    Which otherwise would vibrantly enrich
                    their communities with
shopping lists
and how busy they are because they have to work
and the things they thought when
the Karen at the
checkout counter
didn't like waiting for me to call my cousin.
          We have so much work to do.

For if the soul is, in fact, dependent
upon the body,
therefore, this
division of the lines upon the page
as they motion the eyes according to
traditional structures of poesy
is an attempt to restrict the narrative
of soul from authentic expression
of experience.
And yet Plato is still taught in universities across the country.
I can't understand it.

The research of R. Rosenberg
clearly demonstrates

That Shakespeare's Othello
Is objectively bad.

The holistic kingdom
itself
is symbolic of white desperation
before irony.
Othello cannot exude in an outward world
because of the color of his skin.
And his mind is easily fooled
by the merchant.
His anger fails to express itself
in the white restraints
of iambic pentameter
and thematic structure.
When he finally commits
mostly-peaceful
murder it is therefore
a triumph
over racist metastructures.
And yet white fragility
clearly mars the play,
for as Jessika D. Williams
states after portraying
Othello, racism "has to do with
how we're doing it
and when we're
doing it."

As this intriguing statement alludes to, the fixed philosophical position of time is contingent upon
new enlightenment thought
which then re-authors the narrative of
Othello into an anti-racist mobility.

Or, in the words of Mx. Rosenlevin, "Roland

Barthes outlines a phenomenon he calls annulation, or annulment: an 'explosion of language during which the subject manages to annul the loved object under the volume of love itself: by a specifically amorous perversion, it is love the subject loves, not the object.' This undecidability as a fragmentation of theme disseminates with analystic precision the desubjectification of guilt on the part of Shakespeare's contemporaneous audience-voice. For, if Iago is understood as a hidden marrano, the titular Othello's decision to murder is truly a murder of the différend active in the play's metastructure. And you can see the effect of this recurring thematic rape on the self-image of underpriviliged and minority children in their engagement with Shakespeare. These ironic pre-conditions applied, the theatrical simulation reveals the depthlessness of white literature, and re-transitions the narrative into the realm of the subjective good."

II

Evelyn Greene's brave deconstruction of traditional criticism,

especially in Yeats and Eliot,
would finally, in the year 2022,
give the black voice of
the female poet Leticia Jackson its
due accolades, long after she
was made Poet Laureate
and drove an Escalade.

the groundbreaking epic poem *a bird*, jackson's finest achievement in *ur enough*, displays the harsh realities of internalized segregation. the poem is included here in its entirety. remember to subscribe to mx jackson's patreon and onlyfans.

i tried
to sing.
But could
'nt.
there was songs
i heard em,
them songs,
but they wasn't good
to me
and I tried
to sing
the billowing
curtains of my self
on the page of life

but my voice was like
the dreams we aren't allowed to have
and
when the wind
motions the curtains
with the energy
of a knowing gaze

we wonder
when we can sing.
and kiss
the air
and curtains
with sweet dreams
and the lies
a secret betrays.
—Leticia Jackson, *a bird*

Astounding in its liberation from relevance authority, Jackson's epic poem calls to mind the profundity of *Litany in Which Certain Things are Crossed Out*:

Every morning the maple leaves.
Every morning another chapter where
the hero shifts
from one foot to the other. Every morning the
same big
and little words all spelling out desire, all spelling out
You will be alone always
and then you will die.
So maybe I wanted to give you something more
than a catalog
of non-definitive acts,
something other than the desperation.
Dear So-and-So, I'm sorry I couldn't
come to your party.
—Richard Siken

or Mark Leidner in his groundbreaking work, *I'm Running for President*:

i believe every dog turd is a sundial
when the sun is out, and when the moon is out
every buffoon is a poet, and wisdom is anything
an idiot will pay to find out
no matter what heavenly body is visible

Greene goes on to discuss the importance of *Blood on the Fog* by Tongo Eisen-Martin:

"Reminiscent of June Jordan in their near-embrace of violence, these poems have a powerful ambivalence about what effect they might have in the world; they are very aware of being poems: "A non-future dripping with real people/I mean, real people ... Not poem people." "I write poems today/I kill america today." "Has the poem started yet?/I will tuck your shirt into the earth." The language is visionary, sometimes trancelike. "It takes a violent middleman for me to talk to myself." "I'm sorry to make you relive all of this, Lord... Lord, is that my revolver in your hand?" "I am weak first/Before anything, I first become weak." "there goes the poet — killing without killing — don't mind this."

Which brings us
nicely in narrative accumulation to

III
Taika Waititi and Thor's Search for Self

We are given over to absolute solitude. No one can speak with us and no one can speak for us.
—Jacques Derrida

In Taiki Waititi's breakthrough art film, *Thor: Love and Thunder*, we see that Ezra Pound's modern attempt to show that myths are, in fact, about the self, and the actual life we live, is a failed experiment.
RIP.
Thor's ability to divest the other of agency in order to occupy his own feeling in the matter, to showcase his own suffering, makes the matter clear. We hardly need to expand this point.
The film's utter failure as a narrative inevitably reveals itself an heir to the work of Paige Lewis, especially in her epic poem, *Yael*:

"Sometimes, when they think of Heber away at war, Yael grows giddy, presses their smile hard into their pillow until the whirling joy subsides. But what is the mainspring of that giddiness? They try to dissect the thought:

Heber = Giddy

Or

Heber away = Giddy

Or

Heber away at war = Giddy"

Like Yael, Thor's motivational throughline is
weak.
Which brings us, in conclusion, to the question to which our efforts must divert themselves:

what is poetry, anyway? i mean, really.

This is a shocking claim in the age of the Anthropocene, yet through self-imposed hierarchical deconstruction of aesthetic standards, we may see that, if you really think
about it,
in the right way,
a poem that is objectively bad can be subjectively good. This subordinates the injuries of the intersubjective while dethroning the regime of beauty supremacy. For these reasons and more we must stop forcing Shakespeare and the hidden rape alluded to in Keats' *Ode on a Grecian Urn* into our lesson plans when the erotic theater of Ocean Voung's poems about sneaking out of his house to give old men handjobs will accomplish more in the self-making and framing-mechanism essential for modern audiences.

Winter Sketch—ix

Winter, and winter still, and then again;
Do you yet think this wondrous wall-stone crumbling,
Or these arch-gates toppling are yours to save?
The work of giants wastes away and Earth
Has the mighty makers in its hardened grasp.
So seek not a peace in these disordered times,
It will not accrue to thee.

Winter Sketch—x

Kingdom to ruin,
the land so dead and desolate
no flower ever opens
nor river flows.

Lost is the voice
which once toned from many wells,
so the maidens who there dwelled,
their aid forgot.

And yet at moonrise
on many lonesome nights astounded,
I hear the lamentation build
and see her rise.

Her hair flows loose;
a chaplet of blossoms binds her neck;
her slender waist beneath tresses
which skirt the ground.

A candlestick
of gold she carries forth to me.
The burning taper lights her breast
and woeful eyes.

Hopeless for care
is a land when such women loose
solely in dreams the restoring waters
stifled by daybreak.

Winter Sketch—xi

Men keen of heart and wise of spirit,
looking upon, turning and holding
a golden ring of doubtful origin.

Good lords and true, to bondsmen dear;
athwart the centuries I poise
to witness the bright sight unfurl their eyes.

I speak after them, 'shun such gifts!'
But my words falter and fail
as sickly smiles widen their mouths.

Years turn, and centuries; old ways
forgot, so knowledge earned through strife;
sin, decadence, and pride seep through the people.

Now I must heed their issue homilize
on modern progress, for their homes are warm
and they are safe from mortal fear.

Winter Sketch—xii

Now the pale sun towers once more to gleam
Out of the East, like a songless moon
Over this bared expanse and out-worn model,
This abundance nearly lapsed of account;
To light, yes—and to betray these disrobed boughs,
Divested by that same sun of their leaves;
To glow without warmth, so like a faithless creed
Before which we kneel, hailing, "Ah! The light
Of the truth." Such we are beneath this glare—
Abject actors who cannot attain
The most meager of all artistry. This
Is winter.

How somberly the moon
Had toned upon the snow at Christmas.
Surely the spring must come again.

Winter Sketch—iii

Come at length—
august of countenance,
enveloped with rich cloths—
the enfeebled king.

Four servants
lay his wrecked form by fireside;
his hands emerge to warm
by the bright blaze.

Saith the king,
"Approach, friend, be not frightened.
Take this seat beside me;
you are quite safe."

He makes to rise,
and I've endured this presence
ample nights to know
he never shall.

Sallow and moist
with sweat, he again assays
the task to mount an elbow,
but shivers with pain.

What wound has marred thee, king?
And how to soothe and remedy
the relic of thy once noble form?

Leaving Ogygia ii

There gathered a mass of clouds over the stirred
And suffering sea, as blustered every wind,
Concealing both land and deep in joyless ash—
And night rushed down out of the heavens.

Out of nightfall—how many twilights, woven
By such ill hands—have I only desired
A passage. And now, all the goddess warned
Seems true. I, and a man of Greece, to bleed
Every damned isle, known and unknown upon
The damned sea; I, who glory wrested
For the gods of my fallen people;
Who has sighted wonders and horrors beyond
The limited scope of the lesser men
Of this low world; I, who alone have seized
A myth from death! All to be but a dim-eyed
Effigy, possessed to blunder
Against my will to the last shorn thread
Of this sick tapestry. That I had died
Before the walls of Troy, before I'd known
The hate for me that gods have seemed to bear!

As he spoke thus, a great wave overwhelmed him,
Rushing a terrible heft, which set whirling
His raft upon the sea. Far from the spars
Was he then tossed, and the rudder drifted
From his hands to be swallowed by the waves,
As he himself was finally engulfed.

Nor could he emerge from the mighty mouth
Of the deep main, for the garments Calypso
Had woven weighed and hindered the man beneath.

Interlude on the Art of Poetry iii

Then Angantry sings:
Hervor daugther
Why do you call me
With evil runes?
You draw a curse down upon you.
Mad you have become
And bereft of reason
That you seek to awaken the dead.
—*Hervararkvida*, translation R. Boyer

Let us discuss the transmigration of souls.

The issue of true revenants is—and must remain—the dominion of the artist, pursued within, via communion with the dead, evidenced solely in his work—"'therefore' is a word the poet must not know." Yet it is possible after some analysis to infer true revenants in delineating aspects of the false—which are known instinctively in intimations.

Of false revenants, I perceive two types: those spirits which, of their own volition, make immediate appearance upon the earth, and, secondly, those souls later ripped from the afterlife through necromancy. As the modernists deal with the former to an obsessive extent, it is to the latter—souls summoned—which we must direct our discourse.

It is clear today to all, and to even the worst of readers, that contemporary poetry has lost the art of communing with the dead. Most would-be poets have simply thrown up their hands and declared the words of the past unworthy of enlightened ears. Others, perhaps doing equal harm, dedicate their art to necromancy.

My lament is hardly unique. Yet seldom have I seen any true attempt to discern what precisely is the matter with contemporary poetry. Yes, one hears grumblings of the receding sea of faith, of the spread of consumerism, of decrescent attention spans, and, of course, of Marxist social utility—yet these attempted explications seem to fall short of defining the true problem, and we may understand each as mere symptoms of a broader illness within the ethnos.

Worse, the poetry of those who have offered such complaints universally mirrors the failure of that very verse which they claim to deride, for the work of the necromancer is polar with that of the atheist. From the New Formalists to the writers and editors of *The Society of Classical Poets*, I see no discernible difference between this hated postmodern poetry and the work of its critics. Explore Leo Yankevich's lines of Ashberrian nonsense in his *Paean*—

> A blue elf's smile on the surface of milk
> in a bowl is pleasant delirium,
> much nicer to look at than blood on silk,
> than a spider bellowing kingdom come.
>
> If I could understand the words of wood,
> crucified with nails, I'd say that it hurts
> to be wood, but wouldn't be understood
> except, perhaps, by lizards wearing skirts.
>
> The world's so definitive, there's no room
> for gnomes and angels, for nymphs without clits.
> Yet, a few men have existed for whom
> trees walked in perfect accord with their wits.
>
> This poem in part is written in their praise

and for the bright Light that never decays

Can such ostentatious originality—how precisely may a spider "bellow" kingdom come?—originate from a studied correspondence with our poetic tradition? Is it merely in the shock of surprising image and word choice that Shakespeare or Crane deliver power into their words? What sense connects these disparate images into a discernible poem, as poems of the past were expected to possess? Furthermore, how did the late Mr. Yankevich know when to conclude his lines, if they are not of a regular meter? Did he truly, as it seems, simply count syllables to ten?

To my mind, Yankevich, however noble his intentions, worked with an utter disregard for tradition. Yet there is at least talent in him. The soulless and broken lines of his poems seem artfully to represent the desolate streets they describe, which then seem to resemble the apparent soullessness of our Modern world as it remains in post-war flux. No, Yankevich is not the worst offender among "traditionalists."

Joseph S. Salemi of *The Society of Classical Poets*, whose essay *How to Write Classical Poetry*—which is sadly only available for the steep price of $19.99—aims to instruct the laymen on the composition of traditional poetry, with a concentration on Iambic Pentameter. However, this supposed torchbearer once composed and, worse, chose to publish the following poem, *The Fates Give Oedipus a Consolation Prize*—

Oedipus, Oedipus, it won't be said of us
That we abandoned you, blinded and frail.
Say that you're sorry for banging your mommy
And we'll set you up with some fabulous tail.
Sure, you can't see her, but that's immaterial—
You can still function like any good male.

In order to expedite amorous pleasantries
We've had her undies embroidered in Braille.[1]

Even in the second and third lines, in which the meter corrects itself after a metrically confused commencement, there is some greater failure to grasp what it is which makes poetry "traditional." Perhaps Mr. Salemi would claim his ribald fashion an heir to, say, the work of Robert Herrick or Jonathan Swift, yet, even in their lowest, such poets retained a dignity in their words, such as in Swift's *The Lady's Dressing Room*—

So, things which must not be expressed
When plumped into the reeking chest
Send up an excremental smell
To taint the parts from whence they fell:
The petticoats and gown perfume
And waft a stink around every room.
Disgusted Strephon stole away
Repeating in his amorous fits,
Oh! Celia, Celia, Celia shits!

It is in the irony of the sudden appearance of revolting lines in an otherwise dignified work which lends comedy to ribaldry, and it is precisely the absence of a traditional tone which marks Salemi's work as unreadable. Surely then it is not merely in meter and the use of conventional figures that we have lost at least two generations to utter failure.

Salemi's *The Society of Classical Poets* offers an annual contest which aims to recognize the greatest poems composed throughout the year. A *Society* favorite, Joseph Charles MacKenzie received this year's

1 **Oedipus**. Jesus, Mary, and Joseph. One cannot even laugh at these poets. *The Formalist* decided to honor Mr. Salemi's work and publish *The Fates Give Oedipus a Consolation Prize*—and that, friends and neighbors, is cause for despair.

prize (2020) for his poem, *Song of the Rose*—

The rose awakens, ere the sky
Has wakened to the sun;
And we, my one true love and I,
Awaken with a tender sigh,
To love until the day has run
And all our pains are done.

We part the burdens of the breast,
The weight of passing cares,
And gather roses, take our rest,
And count the ways that we are blest,
Each offering the other's prayers,
In our old hymns and airs.

For, the sky looks down upon the rose,
The stars upon the sky, and God
On all things, and our hearts He knows,
And Fair Love's face will He disclose
To those, in silk or leather shod,
Who soar, or search or plod.

As Yankevich, MacKenzie is certainly not bereft of talent—though Yankevich is the greater power. Mackenzie's tone is measured, yet immediate; he retains a strict meter yet never strains words nor offers throwaway adjectives in order to fill space. He even—shock of all shocks—retains poetic forms of his own creation throughout his pieces. Yet one is never quite satisfied in reading his work, and many have mentioned detecting something of charlatanism in MacKenzie. This discontent in the reader is, in my analysis, due largely to the poet's failure to properly compose, modulate, and conclude a poetic image—and, of course, low necromancy.[2]

On occasion I am approached by young men whose dream it is to become a poet and who seek advice in beginning their pursuit. Once having offered some words on sacrifice, abandonment, resolve, and proper study, I direct these potentials to the study of poetic images in Percy Shelley, especially *Mont Blanc: Lines Written in the Vale of Chamouni.* The aforementioned work begins with the exploration of a particular image—a waterfall in the awe-striking Alps—chosen by the poet to reflect one precise and well-suited series of ideas and inclinations: to guide the course of his reflections, which never stray from the poem's central image. *Mont Blanc* begins—

> The everlasting universe of things
> Flows through the mind, and rolls its rapid waves,
> Now dark—now glittering—now reflecting gloom—
> Now lending splendour, where from secret springs
> The source of human thought its tribute brings
> Of waters—with a sound but half its own,
> Such as a feeble brook will oft assume,
> In the wild woods, among the mountains lone,
> Where waterfalls around it leap for ever,
> Where woods and winds contend, and a vast river
> Over its rocks ceaselessly bursts and raves.

Returning to MacKenzie's award-winning poem, let us ask: what precisely is the core poetic image of his piece?

> The rose awakens, ere the sky
> Has wakened to the sun;
> And we, my one true love and I,
> Awaken with a tender sigh . . .

2 **necromancy**. Poor Mr. Frost, take again your rest.

The first stanza focuses the reader's imagination on an image, trite, yet so full of potential that great poets across generations have explored this same link: that of two lovers and a rose. In proper usage then, the poem would continue exploring this metaphor. MacKenzie's first two lines of the second stanza offer such a potential exploration, yet the poet neither concludes these reflections nor does he make use of the contemplative momentum to then propel his reader into a further study of the metaphor; instead, MacKenzie abandons his central image entirely. In the third stanza, *Song of the Rose* shifts to an entirely new and utterly unrelated image: that of the Christian God looking down upon all things from His Heavenly seat. The poem then concludes with an incidental statement on the unity of the rich and the poor before the Lord of Heaven.

This unraveling of the poem's central image marks the piece a failure, for all its potential, and discloses the poet's neglectful communion with poetic tradition.

Despite such fundamental missteps in the works of Ashberry, Yankevich, Salemi, and MacKenzie, these poets, and others precisely like them, we are told, are among the best composers of traditional poetry over the past decades; they are the writers who have carried forward the torch of English poetic tradition, which was once held by the great masters of the form.

I see not even a brief glance backward in the work of Ashberry, Yankevich, and the like; yet it is this very glance back, this studied conversation with those who came before, which is the hallmark of that poetry we refer to as "traditional," which serves to dissever communion from atheism and necromancy—a communion which is evidenced in a direct lineage through The Pearl Poet, Shakespeare, Milton, Donne, and forward through the centuries to Crane and Frost.

Winter Sketch—xiv

You, purple-wingéd god of the north wind,
Born of bare-bosomed Eos
From her rosy bed—

Swift down from mountain,
Joyful of heart, with icy breath—
With fervent shoulders heave,
Make moan the sea,
Whip through grassy reeds,
Pack drifts of snow,
Open by force the sky,
And terrify the world.

THE WHITE GODDESS

On The Obsolescence of Oracles

A story has been told of times long passed,
When, through the primal mists, there took to flight
An eagle and swan from the earth's utmost regions,
That they may reliably discern the omphalos;
And each, having at last sighted the other,
Rested upon the rocks where later built
Mortals the temple of Apollo Pythius.
For many years had this fable pronounced
Itself through the inquiring hearts of men
When Epimenides—desirous of
Some certain truth—sought out the Oracle,
To attest, if she may, to the verity of
The ancient tale; yet, having but received
An obscure and uncertain answer there,
He composed in his doubt these verses:

Now do we know that there is not, of earth or sea, a navel;
Yet, if there be, it is known not to mortals, but to gods;
And gods, beyond the sun, are not now known to anyone.

Yet very likely did the gods repulse
The man from his design, and cloud the message
Of the Oracle, for his hubris to inquire
The proof of such a tale, as though he meant,
As with a painting, to test of its virtue.

Translated and adapted from Plutarch's *Moralia*.

Winter Sketch—xv

No longer may we pursue a certain impress
Trod through the prairie, nor the distant thunder—
Yet across the treeless slope—where reedy grasses
Suffer the snow—may we in wandering
At last site the ascending smoke where huffs
A lone buffalo before the barren plateau.

Leaving Ogygia iii

Near to the man upon the deep's vast bosom,
The fury of the tempest had calmed.
Then to the placid surface rose the guardian
Of all men who would dare the unstable sea,
The white, suppliant waters rushing
Upon her serene and recumbent visage.

"Unhappy man, why does Poseidon trouble
The sea about thee and stir thee such woe?
For all his rage he shall not yield and loose
Thy soul to its rest. Only do thou thusly—
Thou seems not witless—cast these garments
Of Calypso's fashioning and cede thy raft
To the winds and the sea. Swim with thy hands
And strive toward Phaeacia, where thou may
Finally escape thy woe. Take now this veil
To stretch beneath thy breast. It is the work
Of gods and will stave off even thy fear.
Yet when thy hands have touched the breast of land,
Cast then this veil to the receding tide
To drift afar, and turn thyself away."

Thus speaking, Leucothea gave her veil
And slipped herself again beneath the waves.
Yet to his fear did the man yet cling, thus
Would he not obey the wisdom of the goddess.

Winter Wind

Whose captivated hand first graphed
On freshest scroll of wind his seal,
To alter with his secret craft
Unfathomed life to inner real?

Listen with care—choicest wonders
Avow the wind, if only one a moment
Will yield his voice. How the mind will lull itself
Away with sweet singing when one is not yet
Weary of the measure. O, I have allotted
Such imperishable wanderings
A dreamy middle-night, as I have lain
At rest in the gentle grasp of silence—
When the proud towers of a lifetime
Bedim to wondrous visitants, and waste
Before my eyes, as always I had known
They in a silent moment would. O yes,
Reign after reign had they outlasted—
Loves and philosophies, the birth of children,
And so many deaths; all performed within
These tumbling spires and empty halls now lapsing
To the night—as the wind moans in a stilling
Song of its own over the earth, and one
Is lost to the whispering whist of the snow
And the wordless designs of arrest.

And the breath of the wind becomes our breath,
And the ghosts of our memories, each a burdened
Wonder of its own, no longer are

But wayward dreams to be recalled in hushed
Moments with such remorse, but whispers
Of an abandoned path, ungraspable
As the recoil of leaves which tide upon
The wind-stirred street, awaiting always
The seizure of voice.

Thus fashion we our temples
To the ever-retreating intimations
Of the wind, greater and more subtle
Than ever upon earth had risen before—
To receive supplication within halls
Of pendant charms, chiming through the aisles
As though roused by the wind; lovely voices
Appealing in ardor, which make us crave
To listen—for a whisper, a pure whisper,
To topple with the force of silence
These cold and obstinate towers within.
And so we pause awhile to hear the songs
They will sing. What man ever has before
Continued on and not listened with intent
To such sweet voices—voices which seem to know
Of all upon the fertile earth; which will leave one
Wiser as he passes through this world
Of suffering; voices which will at last
Reward him with eternal life—in his death.

Winter Sketch—xvi

Softer the snow upon my pane
Than softly glows the sun in wane,
As frosted tendrils to inure
Creep their sullen contour.

Warmly to me she wisps like vapor
From memory's dimming taper,
To once again caress the heart
Grown callous absent of her art.

Winter Sketch—xvii

O spirit who once said,
I lived more with ghosts
Than in her bed—
I hear a thousand poems among the dead.

O spirit who once said,
My work is but a refuge
To which I've fled—
I hear a thousand poems among the dead.

O spirit who once said,
My love is like a skin
Too quickly shed—
I hear a thousand poems among the dead.

And though I listen
And I write, the horror is,
Though all the poems my heart has shed,
Yet still the ghosts fill me with dread—
But I hear a thousand poems among the dead.

Winter Sketch—xviii

As vacant are these streets as is the eye
  Of winter's brooding noon, whose light,
  gray light, the fallen snow imbues.

And idly gleam the concourses within
  Their paneless frames, where once-ascending walls
   A lower realm attain; snow adorned,

The halls open as though some threshold has
  Unsealed its disremembered gate,
  That ghostly time may, whispering, mourn.

Interlude on the Art of Poetry iv

I. Resonance

Time has been kind to Percy Shelley, and rightfully so. As Yeats remarked, there was an hour in which the academic perception of Shelley's work bore little more vigor than to state it was "Godwin's *Political Justice* put into rhyme." Hard as it now is to believe, scholars once regarded Shelley as little more than a "crude revolutionist." No doubt our current academia, if such "men and womxn of letters" were ever to read Shelley, would happily agree with this evaluation—after first prefacing their Marxist Utopian ideals with a statement that the poet was, of course, a racist, sexist, and transphobe. But it is not that academia of which I speak. Among today's only remaining true academics, the autodidacts, Shelley's verse is understood to communicate a profound metaphysics. He was, we few now know, a poet of the highest order—not simply for his word choice and rhythm, but for the spiritual depth which, more than the conventional devices of prosody, gave his work form—an intellectual structure that unfortunately does not exist in many of the finest poets, including Crane and, I regret to admit, Pound.

I know a young philosopher who hopes to reinstate this order in his own field. Subjectivity, he rightly claims, is a corner into which modern philosophers have backed, having no intellectual order to mold and guide their thoughts along saner avenues of exploration.

This philosopher once planned an elaborate metaphysical scheme which, once his studies are complete, he intends to write. I do not know what progress he has accomplished toward this dream. Thankfully, however, he did compose an intriguing outline of his system, which he calls Resonant Metaphysics.

Imagine, he wrote in outlining one argument of his theory, a field occupied by millions of weather vanes, with each vane linked to the other via a system of pipes. Every vane would then influence every other. Now imagine, he continued, that each vane possesses a "natural direction" to which it will point absent of outside influences. With millions of vanes and, furthermore, millions of conflicting factors, the movements within the field may seem so random that a bystander would never guess that the weather vanes are all connected and, thus, irrevocably dependent upon one another.

The philosopher's system, to which I may not offer due justice here, reminded me, at the time of my first reading, of the work of the Presocratics. Viewed from a void, as it were, Resonant Metaphysics is a fascinating oddity. One can hardly see an entire people grabbing hold of the concept as a uniting force—yet viewed in tandem with a series of other metaphysical systems, at times contradictory, at times unified, one would bear witness to the reincarnation of an entire field of thought. I can hardly overstate the benefits of such a movement. And yet again, the philosopher's early work lacked one essential detail which withheld the man from the achievement of his dreams: he needed first to immerse himself in a thorough and dedicated study of the great men of the past in order to understand the forms of philosophy itself. It is a detriment to the general welfare when such men falter at this basic step—sadly, a common occurrence.

Doubtlessly, there are many poets at work this very instant, each laboring under the desperate hope that they, or at least another, will save their own field. I have, in fact, encountered a few myself. Each of them, just as the philosopher—though less talented in their profession than he—have faltered in the very same initial step. This failure has only served to deepen the winter which chokes not only poetry or philosophy, but all areas of life at this unfortunate moment in time. For not only are we now deprived of the work of these few capable of providing it, we are instead offered their work in twisted, embryonic forms—often shaped by necromancy or artistic atheism.

II. The Outdated Forms of Bygone Eras

It was a young college professor and widely published poet who once set my mind on the problem of poetry's recent failure. Upon sharing some of my admittedly youthful poetry with this woman, she at once commented, "I wish I could kill the old dead white guys in your head."

From this I concluded she believed my work to be stale and lifeless. When I inquired into particulars, wondering what, if anything, I could do to improve my attempts, her first mention was of meter. Meter, she claimed, sapped poetry of its energy, and was, furthermore, the relic of an aristocratic monopoly of art, in which barriers, in her thinking, were set to preclude the artistic presumptions of the downtrodden.

I offered no argument and thanked the woman for looking into my attempts, yet a dozen questions raced through my mind. How is it one may read such poets as those of our literary canon—so many of whom made use of Iambic Pentameter with such immediacy, experimentation, and passion—and yet believe those works of art lifeless? I felt rather indignant on this matter, as the guiding voices of my youth, far from seeming "dated," appeared to me as men of unsurpassed wisdom and intensity. Furthermore, I would say in my many inner debates, what precisely is poetry if it has no discernible meter? Must not there exist a definitive separation between this art and that of prose? Must there not also exist some fundamental forms, gradually perfected over the centuries? Furthermore, when should one conclude his lines if he makes no use of meter? Whenever he wishes? May have this absence of rules and guidelines contributed greatly to the unrefined voice and imprecise wording of the postmodern poets? On and on I went, yet I did not set myself to the task of dealing properly with these and other concerns.

Some years later, I shared a more mature—though still lacking—series of poems with a poet laureate. I did not particularly admire his work, but he seemed talented and, considering his advanced years—he has since passed—I found myself eager to receive his reflections.

For weeks I waited, scrutinizing with longing the title and address of each email in my inbox. It is with only a little shame I admit that I hoped for a response akin to that famous letter a great American poet once received in quite similar circumstances.

After some months, the poet laureate finally offered his thoughts, for which I am eternally grateful. Having first extended some encouraging words regarding my artistic potential, he began, inevitably, to discuss meter. Meter, he claimed, would forever prohibit the proliferation of my work. After all, the poet went on to say, such devices fell out of popular usage in the far-off days of the "middle of the 19th century." His e-mail concluded with further kindness and a grave reminder: I must learn to write in the contemporary fashion if I am ever to be read.

This evaluation, along with its mistaken timeline, baffled me. My work yet lacked a Shellian system, and these first dramatic monologues were far from the early work of Pound, but could such artistic leaps occur at all without first mastering the art's foundational forms? Must I truly, as he seemed to imply, not only discard meter, but lower my voice into that of the mundane prose usage of daily life? All of this was indeed frustrating, yet it did not sway my resolve; in fact, the many pertinent questions of my college days returned with a greater clarity—for this my gratitude persists.

III. Torchbearers of Tradition

At about the time of my correspondence with the laureate, I discovered—in my search for poets and critics possessing the adequate taste and education to offer a proper response to my work, for good or ill—an online subculture centered around the writing and publishing of traditional poetry: specifically, the *Society of Classical Poets*, those supposed "diviners by the dead" which we have discussed at length. Based out of New York, the *Society*'s stated mission is to "reestablish poetry as one of the most widely appreciated forms of literature . . . [and] to support poets who apply classical techniques in modern poetry through publication and performance opportunities and awards . . ."

One can imagine the thrill I experienced in reading

such a statement. I at once set myself to submitting my blank verse translation of the prologue to Gottfried von Strassburg's epic, *Tristan*.

The *Society* accepted the piece for publication and readers may now encounter my translation on the *Society* website. Yet this publication's editors did offer some fascinating criticism—not of the quality of my words, nor of my translation, but, again, of meter. It seems the *Society*'s editors believed my work to lack a proper meter.

In my wide reading of that English verse composed since the invention of Iambic Pentameter, the beauty of our versification has seemed to exist not merely in the rigid adherence to the iambic foot, but in the appropriately timed and rule-based substitution of iambic feet with some few agreed upon unconventional units. No great poet, at least of whom I am aware, failed to make use, for example, of the choriamb, third epitrite, the minor ionic, or feminine ending. In fact, the father and very center of English poetry experimented even further, often including anapests, a short feminine ending, epic caesuras, and, as in the sixth line of the excerpt below, the occasioned dismissal of an opening unstressed syllable, often referred to as a "headless iamb."

> I had forgot that foul conspiracy
> Of the beast Caliban and his confederates
> Against my life: the minute of their plot
> Is almost come.
>   Well done! Avoid no more!
> This is strange. Your father's in some passion
> That works him strongly.

His experimentation then echoed, at times brilliantly and at times poorly, through the work of Milton and others. In this vein, the creators of free verse justified their keen experiments in prosody. As seen in Whitman and Crane, their work was far from the free-for-all that we know free verse as today—

> A noiseless patient spider,
> I mark'd where on a little promontory it stood isolated,
> Mark'd how to explore the vacant vast surrounding,
> It launch'd forth filament, filament, filament, out of itself,
> Ever unreeling them, ever tirelessly speeding them.
>
> And you O my soul where you stand,
> Surrounded, detached, in measureless oceans of space,
> Ceaselessly musing, venturing, throwing, seeking the
> spheres to connect them,
> Till the bridge you will need be form'd, till the
> ductile anchor hold,
> Till the gossamer thread you fling catch somewhere,
> O my soul.
> —Walt Whitman, *A Noiseless Patient Spider*
>
> And yet this great wink of eternity,
> Of rimless floods, unfettered lewardings,
> Samite sheeted and processioned where
> Her undinal vast belly moonward bends,
> Laughing the wrapt inflections of our love;
>
> Take this Sea, whose diapason knells
> On scrolls of silver snowy sentences,
> The sceptred terror of whose sessions rends
> As her demeanors motion well or ill,
> All but the pieties of lovers' hands.
> —Hart Crane, from *Voyages*

Despite the abundance of substitution within our literary canon, the editors of the *Society of Classical*

Poets were discontent with my failure to conform to their apparent philosophy of Five Iambs Per Line. Once again, it seemed my search had failed, despite the publishing of my translation. In my initial wonderment over this issue, I began researching the work produced and published by the *Society*. With some rare exceptions—which often read as simple mistakes—I discovered that very same stale and infertile poetry the professor and the laureate seemed to crusade against: pastiche, in rigid and thoughtless adherence to the misunderstood rules of bygone eras, as though some well-intentioned and curious seeker had, of his own accord, discovered the ruins of an ancient temple and, within, found there the scraps of some forgotten holy text; and who then, in his awe, imagined himself an adherent to the once-revered customs of a lapsed people. In other words—necromancy.

IV. Unity of Subject and Form

The writing of a novel and the composition of a poem—whether a brief lyric or book-spanning epic—are clearly separate arts, and the definition of this separation should be the subject of an entire series of essays rather than the goal of a single entry, yet it is precisely this matter of definition which swims the inner waters of my mind when I consider the value of writing in meter.

As Frost claimed, "writing free verse is like playing tennis with the net down." What the great poet's statement alludes to is the presence of meter in the very concept of poetry: poetry is, at least partially, defined by the presence of meter and predetermined structures which aid the poet in elevating the written word from the mundanities of daily usage which, through familiarity, are sapped of their potential vigor.

The application of a meter is one of the central methods which allows for this elevation of words into something novel yet timeless, to then draw the focus of a reader's mind into concerns beyond those of his daily bread, in a language which begs the tongue to speak aloud with a tone and rhythm which seem to emanate from something or someplace holy rather than from the ego.

The art, or subject, of the novel, and of all prose writing, contrary to poetry, is the exposure of the day-to-day by the setting of our experiences in plain language before our eyes, for us to then evaluate with an appropriate distance—a distance from which we may view the beauty, sublimity, folly, and heroism of our lived experience. The novel is intended to mirror the language of man's daily life, whereas the intent of poetry is to elevate language into a beauty or sublimity of its own power.

Meter is far from the only tool a poet must use to achieve this effect, yet it is central to the poetic endeavor: a focused, rule-based, expressive meter begs the poet to consider the musical and syllabic value of each word, rendering the language new, even for the poet. When we rid the poet of meter, we rid poetry of an essential boundary which keeps the words from slipping into the day-to-day usage of prose, where the power and beauty inevitably falter. For proof of this, examine the tradition-less "poetry" written and published since the middle of the 20th century. Those poems which do not cascade into nonsense and faux-mysticism, take refuge instead within the mundane—

> They have carried the mahogany
> chair and the cane rocker
> out under the lilac bush,

and my father and mother darkly sit
there, in black clothes.
Our clapboard house stands fast on its hill,
my doll lies in her wicker pram
gazing at western Massachusetts.
This was our world.
I could remake each shaft of grass
feeling its rasp on my fingers,
draw out the map of every lilac leaf
or the net of veins on my father's
grief-tranced hand.
—Adrienne Rich, *Morning Picture*

Rich's writing is lovely. Her reflections inspire with such clarity in the reader's mind the soft comfort of childhood that it seems as though the day-to-day of our own lost years of youth are bare before us, for us to cherish and to then use as a guide in our adult search for peace—just as in prose. Whatever Rich's abilities—which I value, at least in this piece, highly—the only possible separation between poetry and prose in the above excerpt is the division of the work into lines. If I had set these sentences as a short paragraph, would any reader doubt their existence in a vivid novel or short story? This is the language of the mundane, and yet Rich's work is accepted as verse; once having discarded meter, why not simply divide everyday language—prose—into an arbitrary series of lines?

Prior to this current age, poets and critics understood meter's presence at the very heart of poetry—and, no, ye postmoderns, not merely since the Reformation, nor even since the implementation of Iambic Pentameter, but far across space and time, from Europe to the Middle East to the Far East, over the course of millennia. From the Finnish *Kalevala* to the Old Norse *Eddas*, to Homer, and all the way back to Sanskrit and the *Rig Veda*—poetry simply was written in meter, and meter simply was accepted as a defining mark of poetry as such. Without meter's influence, the boundary lines quickly deteriorate to the extent that what is today called poetry contains nearly no definitive characteristics which separate the work from prose writing. How then, having discarded our art's fundamental features, may we elevate our work beyond its most basic expression?

Despite these concerns, writers of poetry—whether it be those tarantulas who hope to erode the characteristics of poetry's past or those necromancers and atheists who believe themselves to be torchbearers of poetic tradition—have failed to properly educate themselves on this essential aspect of their own chosen field of work, and poetry has, inevitably, lapsed from its central position of respect.

In his *A Defense of Poetry*, Shelley claims "Poets, according to the circumstances of the age and nation in which they appeared, were called in the earliest epochs of the world legislators or prophets, and a poet essentially comprises and unites both these characters. For he not only beholds intensely the present as it is and discovers those laws according to which present things are to be ordained, but he beholds the future in the present, and his thoughts are the germs of flowers and the fruit of latest time."

Before the world redeemer may take up his father's sword and perform heroic acts, Jordan Peterson would certainly agree, he must first learn to make his own bed. Today's poet, lacking formal structures and education—encouraged to toss about, motivated by every draft of desire which for a moment pulls at his sleeve—neglected finally to nihilism, finds himself standing before a vast winterscape of formless shapes, seemingly disunited in every conceivable way. Friendship, marriage, family—it is all inconstant. His world takes technological leaps by the day. Not only does he fail to discern what it is he should write, he does not so much as know how to write in the first place.

But those few determined to stand and meet the challenge, those few seekers who have braved the tundra and there received the boon of lost knowledge, must then face the true task—not of ridding the world of its seasons, but rather of curing the bite of winter within the soul. As Joseph Campbell observed, "in doing that, you save the world. The influence of a vital person vitalizes."

I have no more beacons to light your way. I can only offer hope. The deed is worth doing, and it is possible. The stories abound—in myth, classic art, and even the cinema. As the princess of The Three Heads of the Well discovered—signs appear along the way for the one who dares the journey.

One Strike of Lightning

Modern psychologists offer hope to the despairing man or woman, between doses of lithium, in the form of small successes, gained once at a time through 'hard work.' There is no magic, they like to say, which will revive the not-soul. You got out of bed today, and that is a start. You may quell the resentment you hold for your children by first counting to ten and always remembering to breathe. Don't forget to refill your prescription.[1]

Like "forces pulling from the center of the earth" it came back in one strike of lightning. If you are surprised or reticent to believe, ask yourself this: from whence does a poem originate?

It is surely something beyond mere feeling which gives birth to a poem. What emotion could impregnate a man with such lines as, "Hear the voice of the Bard! / Who Present, Past, & Future, sees"? Neither is it the intellect, as any astute reader of Tennyson will acknowledge. It is, as Rilke rightly affirms, an experience.[2] But not just any experience. One's commonplace observations during his daily commute

1 What must surprise in this is how seldom the deniers of all beyond the 'desert of the real' and the language of biological processes arrive, even by accident, at an approximation of truth. Sheer statistical probability ought to be on their side from time to time.

2. "One should wait, and gather meaning and sweetness a whole life long, a long life if possible, and then, at the very end, one might perhaps be able to write ten good lines. For verses are not feelings, as people imagine – those one has early enough; they are experiences." Rilke, from his *Notebooks of Malte Laurids Brigge*, as translated by Stephen Mitchell.

hardly issue forth with the power of worthwhile poetry. No, it is a specific order of experience which produces poetry: a lightning strike of a moment in which the repetition and familiarity of a lifetime are stripped away and once-commonplace forms emit to the senses absent their usual context. Poetry is an expression of the moment of awe, replete with all which compelled toward this one transcendent shock.

There is perhaps only one human experience which I have not yet encountered properly expressed in a line of verse—retaining its essential -ness, its compelling power—and that is the birth of a child.

It is not merely love that we experience in this moment. Nor is it only that a life's driving forces—its will, its fear, all of it—is somehow shifted away from itself and on to another in Schopenhauerian grandeur—though that too is so—it is, when accompanied with appropriate feelings of love and hope, a shifting of the very omphalos: a moment of the highest artistic and spiritual order. Death cannot match it. Before it, success and failure are meaningless. The birth of a child surpasses all—it awakens.

As I held this lustrous presence in my own arms, merely seconds into our world, I was struck as never before. I felt again. I loved again. I saw again. To me, her birth was as bread. Through her birth, I was reborn.

I was, of course, unable to sustain this poetic experience with the same energy as in my younger days. Rather, my vision fluctuated in and out of focus, flashing with the brilliance of youthful poetry one day, swallowed by the weight of adult care another. But there was now hope, and I began at last to write.

There is a sense within my first hesitant attempts, as well as many poems in this book, that perhaps the poetic moment has occurred. However, this is hardly enough to satisfy the inner critic's needs. There is a consolidation of experience, a density of word, a sustainment of concentration which lacks, as in this poem, one of the first following that strike of lightning—

Dakota's Star-Brimmed Vault

I drive her north at nightfall through the buttes and sags,
Through the hummocked treeless tracts of
Dakota's star-brimmed vault,
That my daughter will learn the dark—clear
dark—and stars.

Returning in the night over the last wild hills,
Horizon-stretched, the looming city-glow enfolds
That swelling plenitude of absolute eyes,
Reducing vibrant truth to uncertain words.

Lacking, yet enough to excite the inexperienced poet. Enough to begin. With time, study, and practice—practice not merely of the voice, but of the vision—I improved, as in this piece, composed when my daughter had reached the age of two—

Hymn of Ermengarde at Sunrise

Blushingly appareled in amber-gleamed dawn;
Tossed spritely on, as bloomed magnolia
In the springtide breeze, ardor her tender cast
Buds to elation, as mused flits compel her play;
While 'neath fresh leaf buds, whose new tufts yet hum
Autonomy's luring appeal to summer,
Spring has her face blushingly appareled.

Fountain of beauty, with wonder through the garden

She pours a consecration of regard
As inspired she flits upon grass,
Blushingly appareled.

Joyous drift' lay, the chiming of brook o'er rock
Chants 'cross the grove, "Come, let us sing of sprouts
And buds which lean, brushing diffuse impressions
Upon the gliding water's earnest gleam;
Lilt of the fathomless Elysian sheen;
Hymn o'er the teemed bank, and its florets
Relay with your joyous drift' lay."

Whisking her feet through grass of the out-bloomed verge,
Bright-bloomed of the converging March rain,
She cants her caroling
Joyous drift' lay.

Meadow-through flow, rendering the sapphire throne,
Like emanates growth as a diapasoned tone;
And through the mind beauteous ideal, though dimmed,
Casts verse in blessed voices, as spirit limned.

Nearer, ever nearer I drew. Oh, I could nearly reach out and touch it with that piece. It was, I believe, my first success in both poetic concentration and the proper development of a poetic image—but not at all good enough. The poem still told of a young poet, willing his work into being. And, furthermore, a man too reliant upon the Romantics, as he had not yet found within himself his own order with which to guide his voice.

Worse yet, my spirit rarely poured itself forth into Things with the distinctive power and clarity of true poetry. In spite of the joy and love I had discovered in fatherhood, a shadow would often fall over my mind, dimming the world and directing my vision once more toward an inward gloom. This was, I hoped at the time, a mere reverberation of the despair I'd left behind—or, perhaps, an habitual mode of being that would eventually fade from memory. And yet, in silent moments, a nameless doubt often hung over my inner world, like a shadow cast by a cloud on a sunny day, never completely dissipating but only ever changing in shape.

Life continued on for my little family, more or less content and always brimming with the discovery of new joys. We were soon graced by the birth of a son. Struck once more by the awe of birth and fatherhood, my writing progressed, resulting in the following poem—

Aboard the Fort Lincoln Trolley Along Heart River

Secluded in the soft peace of the trolley,
There recurs to my heart this eidolon
Of you, emerged of that pliant dim remote
Of all remembrance of these first years,
Emanant and defined. Meandering
The prairie course, Heart River glistens
To your vision through the age-relinquished
Covert—aflow.

Look now upon my face.
What reiterations diffuse and so luster
About the tributary's laden glissade,
Where sylphids tour jete their nimble tread
To impress so brief in billowed tufts upon
The rivulet? What mislaid murmurs
Out of darkness pour to plunge you in their gulf,
And abruptly then subside from waking thought?

When I articulate at last in but
These impressioned glimmers, burdened
With such mystery and lapsed from all but you—
This do I welcome, for you now reveal
To me secured, able, remembering.
For this have I suffered the passage
Of all hardship, and wandered through abodes
Of care. Oh, a song of my true self
Could I sing, of the tossing of the snow
On winter nights, when, fettered by the cold,
I walked alone the streets of exile, hung
About by icicles, bereft of friends,
With but my books and the bound voice within me—
Yet unproved. Those who know not of the roaring
Winter and icy wave of winds, who've pleasured
Not in the swan's song, who've sought not the journey
To strive their spirit forth alone, they cannot
Know of the longing in my heart those nights—
Those solitary nights of my yet-stirring voice.

As groves for you take on their blossoms;
As cities grow wondrous; as all the world
Seems new; as eagerly your spirit urges
Forth with the awe and heart for travel
Upon this lonely course, remember—
That I have welcomed this same suffering,
And I have welcomed it that this voice may
Reiterate at last through you.

There would be many more attempts over several years before I would truly discover my art, and even this breakthrough was only the initiation of an arduous journey through more treacherous terrain.

Leaving Ogygia iv

Bounding the steep acclivities which seethed
Upon the deep, some remnants of his raft—
Spars and their fastenings—withheld the sea
From closing upon the man its watery folds.
Beyond the spiring waves, the heavens shook
With thunder. A towering wave advanced
Over the dreadful visage of the ocean,
Aspiring to conceal the heavens,
And toppled upon him, dashing the man
From what remained of his raft, spreading far
The spars over the rush. Yet did he grasp
And mount a final portion, as though to ride
The unstabled canter of the waves to shore.
Then a livid light convulsed the air and water
With ruin, and in his heart the man at last
Relented. Doffing the garments
Calypso had woven, he offered
Himself to the mercy of the untamable
And welling sea, and dove.

L'isle joyeuse

No more stay these sails, but swell them with abeyance
To such elusive gestures as the sea accords,
Surge after each recursive surge, abating
To flood upon each moment's wave the next;
Expectant—heaving perpetually.

As upon the forlorn shores of Cythera—
Where scattered in myrtle and sand lie
Tablets engraved of lovers, whose soft voices
Have whispered into the wind, never again
To be heard—near on the sand rise yet
An array of columns near ruin, tableless
But for the repose of each nutant dawn.
So beyond the ebullient luster
Which sweeps about the coast only to sigh
And recede, there yet sustains and heaves
An intimate depth, unrestrained by vision,
Conceiving of each fertile present,
Yet so vast as to drown this hall of sapphire
From eyes too yielding—before ever ceding
Their witness to the plunge of sun to sea.

No, I seek not a watery temple
To the dissipating crests of my vessel's wake;
Only open to cast me forth, as waves
Each moment will already grasp again,
While yet the deep retains a sense of seizure.

EPILOGUE

Palace of the Snow Queen

I

Useless to me the divers
signs and resolutions
these men proclaim—

women nor wealth, nor frenzy
of unceasing labor, tenets,
nor pews, nor alters—

none have delivered the pledge
to still my furtive spirit
nor cleanse my sight.

And what glimmers may cast forth
when one attends the lustrous
presence of love

surely may sustain
like a fine spray of rain
to thirsty lips,

yet still the wanderer must spill
his sight across the rolling
desert miles.

Such troubles and more fretting
my mind, I sought at last
a sign within.

II

My vision settled fast
on a stream run through dense
and wintry woods.

Untouched, this wilderness,
and pathless; what man alone
may traverse such wild

and not soon find himself
uncertain of the way,
beset by evil?

What hateful nights of cold,
what false ways to perplex
may one find?

It seemed not lifeless
for I clearly sensed my presence
was not desired.

As I fell to anguish
of ever finding there
a resolution,

the specter of an agèd
man from across the stream
rose to my plea.

Stern of face, battle-hardened,
furrowed by time, and draped
with pearly hair,

his genial eyes sought mine.
With a gnarled finger
he beckoned me

to approach over the stream
near to the woods where he
stood in wait.

Sighting a path of rocks
strewn through the brook, I made
to seek him out.

Treading step by step
upon the mossy stones,
I progressed.

Yet no more than midway the stream,
I found myself again
where I'd begun.

Unswayed by this strange failure,
I set to cross once more
with firm resolve.

So breathing deeply the odors
of the stream and the woods,
I surveyed the way.

All but imperceptible,
a shimmering barrier hung
over the water.

I surmised that this trick
had barred my way and hoped
this time to pass.

Near as soon as begun,
I stood once more beyond
the stream from my goal.

The image of that place—
the virgin woods, celestial
in presence,

such as no man had ever
laid eyes on as he walked
the sane earth;

the gushing stream of water,
so pure as to entice
a quenched man to thirst;

and the strange ghost beyond—
all wavered as to fail
and spurn my journey.

A pursuit only just
begun seemed on the verge
of early failure,

and I knew I would wake
with no hope of ever daring
again the voyage.

At this despairing moment,
a shrill laugh throbbed the scene
as from all directions.

There then appeared, more in
my vision than the woodland,
two bitter eyes.

The secret thoughts and fears
none may have known, I felt
them search with ease.

O how they seemed to relish
in the growing certainty
of my failure

and all failures preceding,
in all my private sins,
and in my fate.

I knew not where to step,
but wished to turn and flee
to solid earth.

Before I could so much
as conceive a retreat,
I was struck cold.

The eyes had vanished
and in their place appeared—
disrobed and lustful—

a spiteful queen. She posed
her sensuous form as though
to mock and lure.

How spoiled with sin,
how loathsome with ill will
I felt myself

as I looked with desire
on the curves of her body—
and surrendered

to weakness and disgust.
Just as all warmth departed
from my soul

and hope seemed but a folly
and lie born of desperation,
a voice proclaimed,

"Heed not her cruel deceptions."
Severe yet caring
did the voice seem

as it commanded,
"Drink of the stream's water
and so draw near."

The beguiling image vanished
at these kind words, yet I
remained uncertain

of what steps I should take
and whether I was fit
for the looming trials.

Like one who mounts the precipice
of a journey long devised,
and decisively

bears witness to the danger
inherent to plans which once
were merely dreams,

I looked to the paled form
of that god or king and said,
"Sire, I dare not.

To traverse this place unharmed
one surely must possess
a virtue I lack."

The man then answered me,
"Her hold over you grows
and will not cease

lest ye take some firm action.
Is this cause not the reason
for your passage?

Seldom may man diverge
to such a place as this
but with intent.

So lest ye will a plunge
to doom and cowardice,
drink of the waters."

I thought of the hollow years
behind, destined to echo
and pursue through time;

I thought of the soft faces
of my children, whose father
slumped so from grace—

and knelt before the stream.
With cupped hands I then drank
the icy water.

III

Like a dreamer waking
from his deep sleep, whose wavering
vision will flit

as though between two worlds,
then settle with a sigh on

life's firm reality,

no sooner than the water
passed by my lips to stream
and chill my throat,

the strange domain of wood
and stream took on once more
a substantial aspect.

I crossed the stream with ease,
undeterred by the barrier
which barred me prior.

The agèd man awaited
my arrival near
the forest fringe.

"Are you the one called Wotan?"
I asked the agèd man.
"You bear his aspect."

"If ye will it, then aye,"
the spirit answered me.
"Many names

through your ancestral lands
and over time I've mantled,
as man asserts."

"And the queen who haunted
my approach to this place,
what name is hers?"

With sympathy he answered,
"That, I expect, ye soon

shall know well."

These woods, as I now stood
so near their depths held little
of the strange menace

I had detected there
before my crossing
of the stream.

The song of bird rang through
a lush wood lit with bars
of golden light.

"Put aside these concerns,"
the man spoke, "and walk
with me these woods."

Though certain of the lessons
such as he may convey,
I answered him,

"Sire, that I would well love,
but I have come here with
a certain task."

He nodded then, as though
expecting a request,
and remained silent.

I thus continued, "Where
may I confront the source
and cause of troubles

which haunt my life despite
of joy and love, to leave

my sight bereft?"

By the reserve of his grim eyes,
he seemed to know full well
my purpose.

Without a word he raised
his hand to point through the woods
down a drear trail.

IV

I had anticipated
a journey long and arduous
but soon arrived.

What monstrous boundings
to crash through the brush
which caged my way

I can hardly now say,
nor what creatures lurk
and stalk those woods,

for by the time that I
achieved my destination,
I breathed uneasy

from but the sight of eyes
and growing surety
of hopelessness.

But even fear fled me
when I beheld at last
my journey's end.

Before me towered

a palace fashioned wholly
with slabs of ice.

Like a captain choiceless but
to cede all authority
over his vessel,

I but bore witness as
my legs climbed one by one
the icy steps.

I thus mounted at last
a white arcade before
the palace doors,

no more mindful than the pillars
which around me soared
high as the trees.

No sooner than my hand
reached forward to throw wide
the entryway,

the doors burst open with
a gust of wind, conveying
the snow queen's voice.

Her simple words proclaimed
through my heart with slow surety—
"You desire me."

And again I bore witness
as her nude form appeared
before my eyes.

No beauty fit to incite

the lowest lust may man's
mind conceive,

so delicate and lithe
her slender form, so august
her visage.

Beneath a plea of virtue,
her eyes confessed a lewd
and devious cunning.

Catching my helpless eyes
as they searched over her body,
she shrieked cruel laughter

then said, "Enter my hall
that you may look on me
and heed my words."

V

On high throne sat the queen,
her eyes cast down on me
with clear pleasure.

No hint was left of that plea
I had seen in her aspect
of false virtue.

Now I saw but disdain,
and pride to demand all
obey her rule.

Yet under the cruelty
she seemed to affect,
I saw some trace

betray the queen that offered
a small hope that I may
achieve my aim.

"It is you who has haunted
me through the years," I spoke.
"To what design?"

At my words light departed
up the walls of her hall
to leave but darkness.

As though enraged that I
would question such as her,
her face inflamed.

Yet she was compelled
to answer, "Yes, it is I,
and you know why—

To possess you so that light,
nor hope, nor joy will ever
shine but through me.

O, I hear now your words
though you speak not—'you never
shall take such hold.'

Yet you know not my ways,
nor of the certainty
of my designs.

With every lustful thought,
with your resentment,
and with your anger,

with every wasted day
which slips through your idle fingers,
you become mine.

Trickle by trickle, like
worrying drops upon
a shelf of rock

your will erodes and soon,
o very soon, shall you
be but my thrall."

Her laugh resounded
through the hall with force
to shake the chamber.

From the high ceiling,
ice shards broke free and fell
to crash round me.

On the walls, living shadows
danced to life and seemed
to watch my movements.

Crueler than ever was
her laugh as the palace toppled
all around me.

For all appearances
I was in mortal danger—
yet knew no fear.

Though she may very well
achieve her ends and own
my very soul,

there was yet something false
in her pride, and in her words—
a desperation.

So I walked through the hall,
and turned not once as I
withdrew from her.

VI

The agèd man awaited
me at his place beside
the icy stream.

With a nod he took hold
of my shoulder with firm hands,
and searched my eyes.

I swore an oath to return
and walk with him his woods,
and turned toward home.

AFTERWORD

From the Prologue of Tristan

Grace in your annals with good charity
Those whose good works have wrought prosperity;
For when regard has lapsed from charity,
So will lapse to naught gracious prosperity.

Duty in all hearts naught regards passed purpose,
And duty's art's to wrought all prosperous;
To denigrate the man of dutiful purpose,
Thus, is to design all hearts unprosperous.

Integrity in want is a subtle art;
His right desires I scarce hear man impart.
So the land teems over with men of middling art;
What rightly man wants, scarce man dares impart.

Esteem I maintain for the man who'll attest
Most keen acclaim for desire's keenest interest,
Who virtue marks, thus virtue will attest;
May honor impress his most virtuous interest.

Truth thus affirmed of all men's perfect worth
By the man of firm reserve to boldly unearth
The righteous and vile at their truest worth,
Man's private worth will pardon and unearth.

Equity in acclaim will art divest,
Where to acclaim the art contends to be so blessed;
For when to equitable praise art is blessed,
Profusion in kind will all art invest.

Reverence and praise denied of fit designs,
Their potent promise to neglect declines;
Yet for the broad felicity inclines
All art when reverent praise marks art's designs.

Idealism though wanes with our age's term;
Today teem scholars who the righteous affirm
As vile, and the vile vouch right, who but to affirm
Rightly design, yet to plight assign art's term.

Competence compels proper accord,
Where right to art's phrasing criticism is scored;
When by envy their antiphon is scored,
Both art and criticism will lapse to discord.

Hallowed virtue, how narrow your lay,
And how arduous yet endures your way!
Blessed is he who sustains to sight a way
Which rightly may prevail your path's narrow lay!

Tempered as I am to prudent age by time,
To idly devise of so supple a mold
As this life's span, and in elusion model
My own neglect through the world, would be to devise
With my age in neglect to the term I've borne.
I thusly have this labor undertaken,
To lay before the world, and to solace
All noble hearts—those hearts so dear to my own,
And that world my own heart so keenly regards.
It is a labor not of the common world,
Nor for its common men, who, as I've learned,
Will not endure the heart's most trivial sorrow,
But wish to revel in their impassioned bliss;
May God justly reward such bliss with His!
All I must say and they must hear but meager
Semblance may bear; the lay they course and that
Which I'll convey cannot but course astray.

It is that other way, that other life
To which my labor pleads, which in one heart
Divergent ways may yet concede; which jointly
May bear its bitter-sweet, its dear regret;
Its heart's content, its heart's lament; its dearest
Life, its lamentful death; its lamentful life,
Its dearest death. That life with the life of my own
Lives in a dear accord; to that world would
I cast my life to live in evermore,
And with it be damned, or by it restored.
It is with that world that I've held my term,
It's by that world that I have been informed,
And guided through a life profoundly borne.
I offer then my art, my one true purpose,
My keenest bequest, that the world I love
May win diversion, and abate a time
Its long anguish.

VOCATUS ATQUE NON VOCATUS DEUS ADERIT

Made in the USA
Columbia, SC
16 October 2023

24533799R00086